Mr. Post's Class

by Isabel Sendao
illustrated by Aleksey Ivanov

PEARSON

Scott
Foresman

Editorial Offices: Glenview, Illinois • Parsippany, New Jersey • New York, New York
Sales Offices: Needham, Massachusetts • Duluth, Georgia • Glenview, Illinois
Coppell, Texas • Ontario, California • Mesa, Arizona

It was a morning in early September. The James Madison Elementary School playground was buzzing with activity. There were happy faces everywhere. Anyone walking by might have wondered why the students were so excited, but the explanation was simple. It was the first day of school.

All of the students had stories to tell about their summer vacation. There were all kinds of adventures to relate. For many of the students, it seemed that it had been a very long time since they had seen their school friends.

The first bell rang, and the students lined up to go into the school. The second bell rang a few minutes later, and the teachers began leading the students inside to their classrooms. It was impossible to keep the students quiet. There were too many squeaks from new sneakers and too many giggles from happy boys and girls.

After the teachers led the excited students inside the school, the whispers and giggles continued to echo through the halls. School was back in session.

Everyone in Mr. Post's third-grade class was curious about their new teacher because it was his first year at James Madison Elementary. He printed his name very neatly on the chalkboard, and the students waited anxiously for him to begin speaking.

"Good morning, class," he finally said. "My name is Mr. Post. The first thing I would like to do today is learn your names. Let's go around the room. Each of you should introduce yourself and share something about yourself with the rest of the class. It could be your hobby or something the rest of the class does not know about you."

No one in the class wanted to be the first to speak, so Mr. Post volunteered to start. "As you know, my name is Mr. Post. I really enjoy traveling and volunteering in my free time. Does anyone have any questions for me?"

Suddenly the classroom was full of chatter. "Will you assign us lots of homework?" someone called out. "Are you good at explaining new ideas?" asked another student. "Do you know any fun games we can play at recess?" called out someone else.

Mr. Post replied, "We can talk about those things later in the day. Right now, let's focus on our hobbies and interests. Who would like to go first?"

"I will," a girl in the front said. "My name is Anna. I like to skateboard in my free time."

"Thank you, Anna," said Mr. Post. "Who is next?" Some of the students still felt shy, but after a few others shared something about themselves, it became easier for everyone.

"I'm Jake, and my favorite thing to do is play guitar," a tall boy explained.

"My name is Mila," said a girl with dark hair. "I paint for fun."

Soon everyone had shared and Mr. Post said, "That was great, class. Now let's talk about what you did over the summer."

Mr. Post began, "I spent my summer working on a special project. I volunteered to work with a team of people who help build houses for people who can't afford to buy them."

Some of the students seemed surprised. Jake raised his hand and asked Mr. Post, "But why did you want to spend your summer working?"

Mr. Post smiled and explained to the class, "Well, I really enjoy helping people in the community because it's exciting and satisfying. The work that I do really benefits the community and helps make it a better place to live. Have any of you ever volunteered to help others?"

The class fell silent, but after a few minutes a few students raised their hands.

"Mila, right?" asked Mr. Post of the dark-haired girl with her hand raised.

She nodded yes and said, "I helped out with the summer program at the preschool where my mom teaches. I really liked playing with the younger children and helping them do crafts."

Jake was the next to share. "Sometimes I help my next door neighbor, Mr. Martinez, with his yard work. He is getting older and has a difficult time doing the work by himself. And I really don't mind doing the yard work because it helps Mr. Martinez, and we have become good friends."

Mr. Post smiled as many of the other students shared ways in which they had helped people during the summer.

Then he said, "Listening to everyone talk has given me an idea. Would you be interested in organizing some events this year that would help people in the community?"

Everyone in the class liked Mr. Post's idea. All the students had suggestions to offer. Someone mentioned that the class could start a recycling program to help reduce waste. Another student pointed out that they could help the elderly bring their groceries home. Another spoke of raking leaves for people who weren't able to rake.

Mr. Post was very pleased with their ideas and their enthusiasm. At the end of the day he said, "Tonight I would like you to think about how much time you can volunteer to the project. Tomorrow we'll vote on all your ideas."

Mr. Post's students went home that night more excited than when they had arrived. Everyone was interested in volunteering together in their community. That evening, some of them talked and came up with even more ideas.

The next day the class filled the chalkboard with their ideas for a community project, and Mr. Post decided that *all* of their ideas were wonderful. He surprised his students and announced that they should try them *all!*

Everyone wondered how that would be possible. But Mr. Post explained, "Today I'm going to discuss our project plan with our principal, Ms. Hall. I'll know more later."

After their math lesson it was time for lunch. In the lunchroom the students talked excitedly about what Mr. Post's plan might be.

That afternoon Mr. Post handed out sheets of paper and announced, "Guess what, class? Ms. Hall approved our project! The next step is for each of you to have a parent fill out these permission slips. The sooner you bring them back, the sooner we can get started."

The plan for the project was to make sign-up sheets for people to fill out. Then the students would volunteer for things they liked to do and had time to do. This meant that Jake could help people with yard work or play his guitar for people at the nursing home. Mila could help paint a new mural in the kindergarten classroom.

One day the class was discussing how they should tell the community about their project. A student named Julio raised his hand.

"I think we should make posters that tell the services that we offer. Then people could fill out sign-up sheets," he suggested.

"Great idea, Julio," Mr. Post said. "We should put the name of our project on the poster too." The day before, the class had decided to name the project "Project Good Neighbor."

Some students created posters, while others made the sign-up sheets. Together, they hung everything up, so people could come in and sign up for whatever service they needed. Some people signed up that very first day!

Project Good Neighbor became a huge success. All the people who asked for help were very happy with the work the students did.

They volunteered all over the community. Some students helped run errands for people who could not do them themselves. Anna taught younger kids all about skateboarding helmet safety. Jake played his guitar for the nursing home residents on Saturday afternoons.

Word spread quickly about Project Good Neighbor. There was even a newspaper reporter who asked to interview the boys and girls about their activities. Mr. Post was very proud of his third-grade students.

When the reporter arrived in the classroom, she saw that photos of the different volunteer activities had been placed all over the walls. Mr. Post had taken the photos while traveling from place to place to check on how the students were doing.

The reporter was impressed with the smiling faces in the photos. As she looked at the photos, the students explained what they had done.

Anna pointed to a photo of her teaching a young boy to properly put on his safety equipment for skateboarding. "He's a much safer skateboarder now," she explained.

Another photo showed Jake playing his guitar at the nursing home. Jake smiled as he told the reporter, "My picture was even printed in the nursing home's newsletter."

The reporter was surprised to learn how well the students had come to know the people they had helped. She mentioned to Mr. Post that she was impressed with the positive comments that community members had made about his students.

After hearing the stories of each photo, the reporter returned to the local newspaper office and wrote an article about Project Good Neighbor. Her boss was very pleased with the article about Mr. Post's students. He was so pleased that he decided to put her story on the front page of the next day's paper!

The school year went by very quickly. Mr. Post's students hardly noticed the months passing by. They were very busy with Project Good Neighbor.

At the end of the school year, the principal, Ms. Hall, gave each of the students a special award for the dedication that they had shown to their community. Mr. Post told the students that he was proud of them for making the project such a wonderful success. He was especially pleased by all the hard work that they had put into Project Good Neighbor.

Getting Involved

Mr. Post had helped to build affordable housing during his summer vacation. How do groups of people go about building affordable housing? Let's take a closer look.

Some states partner with nonprofit organizations. Together they set a goal for how many affordable houses they want to build in a year. These organizations help pay for some of the building materials, equipment, and land. They also help to organize the volunteer labor. The people who will move into the new houses help to build them too. For all these reasons, the costs of building the houses stay low. That means people can afford them!